THE FOODIST BUCKET LIST

100 Edible Adventures from Farm to Fork

Iver Marjerison

© 2017 Iver Marjerison

(2022 Edition)

All materials contained are protected by international copyright laws and may not be displayed, distributed, transmitted, reproduced, published or broadcast without the prior and written permission of Iver Marjerison or in the case of third-party materials, the owner of that content.

You may not alter or remove any type of trademark, copyright, or other notice, from copies of the content.

For use of information contained as source material, credit: Iver Marjerison, author, The Foodist Bucket List: Fort Collins, Colorado.

Inquiries: Marjerison@gmail.com

"There is no sincerer love than the love of food."
- George Bernard Shaw

Table of Contents

Special Thanks To 9
Fort Collins 11
Sections 13
Foodist Bucket List 101 14

I: Eats 19
  The Welsh Rabbit Cheese Shop - Funky Cheese 20
  Choice City - Corned Buffalo Reuben................................21
  Silver Grill - Salmon Benedict & Green Chili Hash Browns..22
  Chopstickers - Pork Bao (Water Fried)..............................23
  Tasty Harmony - Nachos De Ynez 24
  Rocky Mountain Olive Oil Co. - White Truffle Olive Oil 25
  Mexicali - Smothered Sweet Pork Burrito 26
  Fox & Crow - Meat Board..27
  Young's Café - Spring Rolls 28
  Waffle Lab - Mile High Grilled Cheese.............................29
  JAWS Sushi - Jeff Roll 30
  Nimo's - Authentic Sushi 31
  Comet Chicken - The Perfect Chicken Sandwich 32
  415 - When Pigs Fly..33
  The Hot Souce Realm - All the Hot Souce..........................34
  Stuft - The Hangover Burger..35
  Little Bird Bakeshop - Quiche Of-The-Day 36
  Rise - The Stack 37
  Waltzing Kanagroo - Guinness Steak & Mushroom Pie 38
  Maza Kabob - Aashak 39
  Café De Bangkok - Northern Style Curry Noddle 40
  Austin's - Rotisserie Chicken 41
  Tortillas Las 4 Americas - Sack of Fresh Tortillas................42
  Petra Grill - Lamb Kabob..43
  Star of India - Butter Chicken 44

DGT - The Bandito *45*
Pickle Barrel - The Balboa …with AuJus* *46*
FoCo Café - Community-Centric Lunch *47*
Totally 80's Pizza - Awesome Frito Pie *48*
Café Bluebird - Kentucky Corn Bread *49*
Doug's Day Diner - Black Betty Burger *50*
Ginger & Baker - Brunch *51*
Avogadro's Number - Tempeh Burger *52*
Big City Burrito - Potato Burrito *53*
The Crown Pub - Pommes Frites *54*
Jax Fish House - Oyster Hour *55*
Krazy Karl's - Spicy Ranch *56*
Mt. Everest Café - Chicken MoMo *57*
Slyce Pizza Co. - Mac & Cheese Pizza *58*
Back Porch Café - Huevos Rancheros *59*
The Colorado Room - Bison Poutine *60*
William Oliver's - Pint-o-Bacon …with a shot of
maple syrup *61*
Nick's - Burger & Brew Special *62*
Surfside 7 - Wild Boar Corn Dog *63*
Taqueria Delicias - Tacos y Tacos …y Tacos y Tacos! *64*
Saigon Grill - Pho *65*
Hog Wild BBQ - Ribs *66*
Los Tarascos - Menudo *67*
The Twisted Noodle - Loaded Garlic Bread *68*
Lyric Cinema Café - Cereal Bar …and Cartoons! *69*
Fiona's Delicatessen - Tara Lee's A True Honey *70*
JeJu - Chicken Bi-Bi-Go *71*
Sally's Kitchen - Ginger Avodaco Fried Rice *72*
Jim's Wings - RamHot Wings *73*
Taqueria Los Comales - Offal-Taco-Trio *74*
Charco Broiler - The Pepper Bob *75*

II: Drinks 77
Fort Collins - Breweries! *79*
Bean Cycle Roasters - The Kerouac *80*

Social - Traditional Absinthe Service *81*
UNION Bar & Soda Fountain - "White Lightning"
Spirited Shake *82*
Ramskeller Pub - Ram Brew *83*
Harbinger Coffee - The Single Origin Pour Over *84*
Gelato & aMore - Hazelnut Gelato *85*
Old Elk Distillery - Peanut Butter Whiskey *86*
Happy Lucky's Teahouse - 3 Shades of Green..................... *87*
Pinball Jones - Pinball Beer *88*
Ku Cha Tea F- ull Matcha Service *89*
Black Bottle Brewery - Cerealiously Count Chocula.............. *90*
Rocket Fizz - Bizarre Soda *91*
Rio Grande - Classic Rio Margarita *92*
Mo Jeaux's - The Beaver *93*
Lucky Joe's - Traditional Irish Coffee............................... *94*
Trail Head Tavern - Iconic Dive Bar Beer *95*
Town Pump - White Lightening & Toxic Fruit.................... *96*
Elliot's Martini Bar - Colorado Herb...............................*97*
Feisty Spirits - Locally Distilled Whiskey Flight.................. *98*
Horse & Dragon - Sad Panda *99*
The Whiskey - Whiskey Sour *100*
The Copper Muse Distillery - The Capone....................... *101*
The Fort Collins - Beer Immersion................................. *103*
Scrumpy's Cider - Summit Flight................................... *104*
Wilbur's Total Beverage - Wine Sampling *105*
Blind Pig - $1 Mimosa.. *106*
Blue Agave - Margarita Flight..................................... *107*
Golden Poppy Herbal Apothecary - Personalized Tea Blend.. *108*
Cooper Smith's - Sigda's Green Chili Golden Ale *109*

III: Desserts.. 111
Nuance - Single Origin Taster Flight *112*
Copoco's Honey - Orange Cinnamon Creamed Honey *113*
Walrus Ice Cream - Joke Flavor..................................... *114*
Vern's Toffee House - Best-You-Eva-Had Almond
Toffee.. *115*

Rainbow Café - Pumpkin Bread French Toast 116
La Creperie & French Bakery - Perfectly Plain
Croissant 117
Café Vino - Toffee Date Cake 118
Alley Cat Coffee House - Chai Milkshake 119
Cheeba Hut - Cereal Bars 120
Butter Cream Cupcakery - Mini Cupcakes....................... 121
Lucile's Creole Café - Beignets 122
City Drug - European Goodies 123
Mary's Mountain Cookies - Salted Caramel Cookie Ice Cream
Sandwich …with Chocolate Chip Cookie
Dough Ice Cream! 124
Snooze - Pancake Flight... 125
Starry Night - Cappucino Cake... 126
Revolution Artisan Pops - Cucumber Lime Popsicle 127
Churn - Space Junkie Cone 128
Ace Gillett's - Ganache Brownie 129
Me Oh My Coffee & Pie - Seasonal Pie............................ 130

IV: Agri-Adventures 131
Fort Collins' - Farmers' Market Awesomeness.................. 132
The Markets 133
The Cooking Studio - Cooking Class 134
Food Tours! 135
Esh's - Crazy Food Bargins 136
The Cupboard - Treats & (Kitchen) Toys 137
Howling Cow Café - Farm Fresh Latte 138
Ten Bears Winery - Local Wine Flight............................. 139
Jessup Farm Artisan Village - Everything Nice 141
Locally Loved - Farm Adventures...................................... 142
Bonus 143

Names & Doodles... 145
One Last Thing… 146

Special Thanks To

Fort Collins *and the people who make the town such an infectiously happy place, the countless restaurateurs, farmers, chefs, and eaters who have obliged to my relentless assault of questioning, and Chef Cameron Trezoglou for sharing his bountiful knowledge of the local cuisine.*

Colorado State University *for providing me with a foundation for my passion and four years of smiles, the rock star Ag Sciences and Sociology Departments for kickstarting my interest in food, Dr. Gary Peterson and Dr. Ken Barbarick for never making me feel like my stupid questions were stupid, Addy Elliott for being selfless with her advising brilliance, and the much needed solitude offered by the basement of the Behavioral Science building (can someone please explain why the bathroom down there has a shower?).*

The Friends *who made my time in Fort Collins so damn much fun... I'm not listing you all, so deal with it. It would take too long, and I don't want to hear you guys whine about how Sean Hercher's name got listed first, how Zack Hodapp's name got spelt wrong, or why Vince Espinosa made the list even though he disappeared after freshman year.*

My Editor */best friend Kelsey Vlamis, who spoils me with her contagious optimism, unparalleled knowledge of the written word, and superhero-like food photography skills. Check her out: TheHungryThinker.com (@TheHungryThinker).*

Fort Collins

Legend has it that thousands of years ago the food gods, bored with their celestial empire, descended to Northern Colorado... all right, so the story isn't that exciting. Basically, it was established as a military outpost in 1864, and shortly after experienced a population swell thanks to farming potential and the founding of the Colorado Agricultural College in 1870. Since then, the population has grown to an estimated 161,000, and developed a culture rich with music, art, bikes, breweries, dogs, and of course... food.

While the 30,000+ students who attend CSU heavily impact the town's culture, it's much more than just a "college town." In fact, the combination of diverse culture, outdoor activities, and economic opportunities routinely land Fort Collins on lists that celebrate its "livability." But you don't need a BuzzFeed article to tell you that. Go spend a day hiking at Horsetooth Reservoir, tubing the Poudre, biking to breweries, or just strolling around Old Town (the inspiration behind Walt Disney's Main Street, U.S.A.), and the infectious energy of happy people doing happy things is sure to be evidence enough of Fort Collins' spectacularness.

Beyond its bounty of activities, adventures, and events, FoCo also boasts a deliciously diverse food culture. While the craft beer scene is the most popularized, the area also has a rich appreciation for local artisans and farmers, which is uniquely complemented by the celebration of hedonistic edible-delights that can only permeate a college town. However, the most influential factor on the area's cuisine is the community of food lovers... who demand quality, celebrate novelty, and selflessly provide the positive energy and financial support that encourages innovation and brilliance amongst the local producers, chefs, and farmers.

While unfortunately this book promises little in the way of helping you experience the area's plethora of non-edible experiences, it's my hope that as these edible adventures immerse you in the community's beautiful food scene, they are able to simultaneously act as a sort of catalyst to help you find new places, try new things, and meet new people... all in an effort to maximize your Fort Collins experience.

Sections

Eats
Everything from burgers to white tablecloth affairs

Drinks
From boozy to nourishing, a compilation of all things sipped

Dessert
Bizarre to traditional… the who's who of the local sweet scene

Hands-on Adventures
Agritourism, markets, locavore must-dos, and farm-to-table experiences

Foodist Bucket List 101

This book has a conversational tone, is informally written, and lacks the sort of detailed information you'd find in a traditional "guidebook"... because it isn't one! I'm just a guy obsessed with uncovering each and every delicious opportunity that an area has to offer, and enjoy sharing my favorite discoveries with other food lovers. As you work your way through the list, keep these things in mind...

1. Not All Inclusive:
No, I didn't eat everywhere...
This list is not an unbiased ranking of every dish in town, nor does it try to be. *My method is simple: I ask, read, research, and scour the area for the ultimate edible adventures (generally leaning toward less expensive and unique items). I then try them out, and whichever ones spin my head around, go in the book!*

<u>Please note: The items are listed randomly; the page numbers are not "ranks" but merely for reference purposes.</u>

2. Inconsistencies
The food and beverage industry is inherently volatile. Certain dishes come and go, chefs have bad days, and with a town that relies heavily on the seasonal labor of often distracted college kids... lackluster service is capable of striking at any moment. If I lead you somewhere that lets you down, I apologize in advance.

3. Adventure:
This list intends to introduce you to a wide array of experiences that define Fort Collins' unique cuisine. While I list specific items, I strongly encourage personalization and improvisation—you know what you like! Think of this like a food-driven scavenger hunt that you can (and should) tailor to your own desires.

4. No Paid Endorsements:
All 100 items in this book are things that I have personally indulged in, and found to be fantastically-awesome.

None of the items have made the list due to financial compensation of any kind.

5. No Addresses or Color?!
The two questions I get the most, both of which have simple answers. First: You have a smartphone and the name of the restaurant—get creative. Second: obviously color photos would look better, but the book would cost a left arm more. You want to pay a left arm more? Didn't think so. Want color? Get the e-book, follow me on Instagram, or go see them for yourself!

6. Satisfaction
Whether you seek out every adventure, successfully filling each page's box with a fat check mark, or only take the journeys in your mind from the comfort of your favorite chair, this book should leave you (and your stomach) with a sense of satisfaction.

If for some reason it doesn't meet these expectations, let me know. I'm always looking to improve.
Marjerison@Gmail.com

FoCo Foodist
.com

I: Eats

Everything from burgers to white tablecloth affairs.

The Welsh Rabbit Cheese Shop
Funky Cheese

The easiest way to describe this cheese shop is some sort of cross between a carnival and a theme park... except with more cheese and less rides. Seriously though, owners Dean, (his wife) Nancy, and (his brother) Nate have curated a stunning array of different fermented dairy products from around the world, making it a true wonderland for anyone looking to ride the flavor-coaster that is artisanal cheese! For the true taste-bud adventure, tell the cheesemonger (guy/gal behind the counter) on duty that you want a wedge of the "funkiest of the funkiest" stuff they got!

Ohh yeah! Don't forget about their bistro around the corner. Featuring wine, beer, small bites, and of course... cheese!

Choice City
Corned Buffalo Reuben

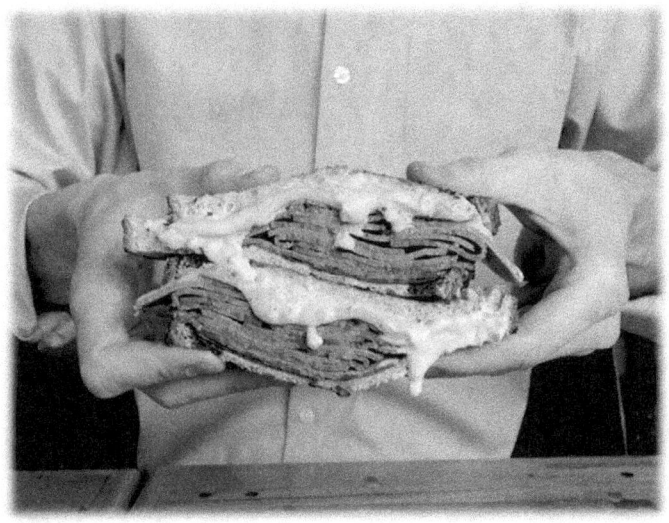

In an attempt to prevent all of the best players from ending up on the same team, professional sports have specific guidelines for drafting players. Luckily for us, the food world isn't like this. Thus, this fast-casual style eatery is able to have the best beers on tap and some of the best minds in the sandwich world crafting a unique menu that boasts a superb variety of meats, cheeses, and toppings. They celebrate these goods with a killer breakfast and lunch menu, and also sell meat off-sale for those DIY types. The drop-what-you're-doing-to-pursue item? The Reuben... with Colorado buffalo meat, homemade 1000 island, swiss, and 'kraut piled high between two slices of grilled rye bread.

Silver Grill
Salmon Benedict
& Green Chili Hash Browns

You don't just become the oldest restaurant in Northern Colorado via dumb luck and mediocre eats. No sir, it takes a sustained flurry of food awesomeness! Stuff like a build-your-own Bloody Mary bar, bottomless thick-cut hash browns, and giant cinnamon rolls (also available in the form of French toast!). Whenever you decide you're in the mood to try out your new favorite breakfast dish, go for this benny—featuring a generous serving of salmon, and a dill-explosion hollandaise sauce.

Tip: *Sub the muffin for a grilled croissant, and get a side of green chili to smother your hash browns in.*

Chopstickers
Pork Bao (Water Fried)

It's like I always say... "The best things in life are steamed, fried, involve pork, and fit in your hand." Okay, fine. I've never actually said that before. But after devouring an entire rack of these things to myself... I just might start! The first time you go you won't have enough stomach space for anything else, but on the second round don't miss the dumplings, and on the third, fourth, fifth, and sixth visits, try everything else! Because this place doesn't miss.

Tasty Harmony
Nachos De Ynez

Hip décor, kombucha by the glass, seasonally inspired cocktails, local produce... and no meat.

Vegan? ...This place is your jam!
Not vegan? ...WAIT!

*I know your mind is reminiscing on your many Tofurky letdowns, but trust me... this place is different. Each dish rocks enough tongue-spinning flavors and palate-pleasing textures that you'll quickly forget their meatless nature—especially with the BBQ Jackfruit on the scene! An act that's nothing short of culinary wizardry, their transformation of this bizarre looking fruit—which you've likely never seen before—represents **BY FAR** the best meat stand-in I have ever had in my life.*

Rocky Mountain Olive Oil Co.
White Truffle Olive Oil

This olive-oil-and-vinegar version of a candy store has dozens of flavors on tap to taste—which is obviously awesome—but let's keep our eyes on the prize... truffles. Long story short, they are goofy looking fungus lumps that grow underground. These fist-sized balls of ugly boast a complexly intense flavor profile that has been culinarily celebrated for centuries. However, the difficulty of cultivation puts the raw stuff at thousands of $'s per pound, making them one of the most expensive foods in the world. For this reason, the essence is usually added to foods via artificially flavored methods. Luckily for your taste buds, this joint has the real stuff! Go for a sample, and if the bizarre funkiness fits your fancy, grab a bottle... your kitchen will never be the same again.

Mexicali Smothered Sweet Pork Burrito

Burrito Euphoria Recipe:

- **1 full:** *made-in-front-of-me tortilla*
- **1 heaping scoop:** *pulled sweet pork*
- **2 fist-fulls:** *cheese*
- **Just enough:** *rice and beans*

Smother the whole thing in an alarming amount of homemade creamy habanero sauce, pass it through a power oven to achieve melty-cheesy perfection, …and nosh!

Fox & Crow
Meat Board

Charcuterie Perfection, Monthly Special Grilled Cheese, Lamb Prosciutto, Happy Cheese, Not So Funky Cheese, Smoked Duck Breast, Wine on Tap... Sooo Much paté, Cured Venison, Blueberry Elk Salami, Killer Happy Hour, Funky Veggies, Pickled Veggies, Water Buffalo Cheese, this place is a manifestation of all that is right with food. to wrap it up;

Young's Café
Spring Rolls

The "Spring Roll" is vague culinary terminology, evolving through time and space to become known within Chinese-American fusion cuisines as a mash of unknowable ingredients, deep-fried in a crispy roll. Generally, they go from a frozen plastic bag to a deep fryer, a shortcut that is not inherently bad, but that does make me appreciate when a place like this goes the traditional route. Their handmade SRs feature pork that's infused with a taste-bud dominating array of spice-forward flavors, and wrapped in a rice paper that is perfectly fried to a crispy perfection. Dining preference? I personally just get a dozen and shoot selfies of myself noshing them in a euphoric state of edible bliss… but technically, I suppose, there are others ways to go about it.

Waffle Lab
Mile High Grilled Cheese

It's safe to say that just about anything smashed between two waffles is going to be a small flavor carnival in your mouth... but the awesomeness of regular waffles wasn't enough for these guys, so they upped the ante by going Liege style. This centuries-old waffle variety is adapted from traditional brioche recipes, that require letting the dough (not batter) rise before cooking. This process creates a richly dense and chewy texture with an outer layer that boasts crisp, caramelized perfection. Now, their sweet waffles are obviously bangin' (S'more?! PB & J?!), but their savory creations are what really get me going. Highly Recommended: add grilled jalapeños and bacon to this generous load of gooey cheese!

JAWS Sushi
Jeff Roll

The story of sushi is long and often misunderstood. The origin can be traced to the packing of raw fish in soured rice as a means of preservation. Once refrigeration came along, the fish packing wasn't really necessary, so it evolved into cooked vinegar rice wrapped around various ingredients—often seafood and often raw. Today, Westerners have gotten a taste for the idea of sushi, but opt for less-than-traditional ingredients, thus creating a fusion cuisine of seaweed-wrapped cream cheese bites, drowned in mayo, that have the sushi elites up in arms. Now, to be fair, I love traditional styles, but I think it's important to recognize the beauty of globalized cuisine! These new-age rolls can't be compared as "better" or "worse"... they're a completely new dish! So in order to embrace this new-age fusion, I like to stray away from my traditional preferences... to periodically experiment with rolls like this!

Nimo's
Authentic Sushi

In contrast to the previous page, this item swings in a more traditional direction, with quality fish being the clear star of every plate dished out. To put it simply: these guys play for keeps, with no catering to the American love affair of deep fried nonsense rolls, and go a step further by actually refusing to serve any "rolls" at the sushi bar. While it may not be typical American sushi dining, the deliberate care and obvious pride that goes into each perfectly adorned clump of rice truly makes this a special experience. I encourage you to embrace this item whole heartedly: sit at the bar, place a few orders of "sushi" NOT "sushi rolls," sip some Sake (bonus points if you get the $300 bottle), and watch the knife-wielding craftsman go to work. Sensory overload, in the most delicious sort of way.

Comet Chicken
The Perfect Chicken Sandwich

@Munchthefood

The average American meat-eater is estimated to consume some 2,400 chickens in their lifetime. Unfortunately, much of that is in the form of lifeless chicken strips and (God-forbid) plain chicken breasts. Luckily for FoCo, there is a cure to the monotony of chicken consumption... and it's this place! I won't even make a sandwich suggestion. Each is better than the last (how is that possible?) and they are all adorned with the perfect combos of sauce and toppings. They also have vegetarian options!

415
When Pigs Fly

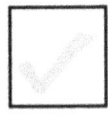

Is it even possible to empirically quantify the flavor-symphony of perfectly-made chicken and waffles?

...the crispy airiness of a masterfully-crafted waffle?
...the subtle citrus-symphony sung by said waffle's orange infusion?
...the sensory overload of a ramekin full of bacon-thyme maple syrup?

Maybe... maybe not. I don't pretend to be versed in quantum-food mathematics. All I know is: opt for the full waffle with double syrup—or be sad.

The Hot Souce Realm
All the Hot Souce

Spicy hot sauce, extra spicy hot sauce, sweet hot sauce, tangy hot sauce, mild hot sauce, extra extra spicy hot sauce, smoky hot sauce, sophisticated hot sauce, chipotle hot sauce, extra extra extra spicy hot sauce, pineapple hot sauce, BBQ hot sauce, jalapeno hot sauce, super smoky hot sauce, saucy hot sauce... THERE ARE SO MANY HOT SAUCES AND NOW I GET TO TRY THEM ALL! (Check their Instagram to find their current locations: @thehotsaucerealm)

Stuft
The Hangover Burger

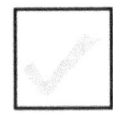

Looking to add some variety to your burger life? ...Then this is the spot for you! Their build-your-own menu offers everything from strawberry preserves to guac, with an equally customizable milkshake menu (go for Mocha-Nutella with a shot of Kalua). Of particular magnificence is this featured item: towering bacon, a fried egg, cheese curds (subbed for cheddar!), on top of a beef patty... drizzled with maple syrup and tenderly adorned between two halves of a glazed donut. Add a side of their award-winning garlic Parmesan fries, and you're in for a nosh-tastic good time!

Little Bird Bakeshop
Quiche Of-The-Day

This bakery seems to have a pretty straightforward food mantra: source locally, cook from scratch... become the quiche champions of the world. All of which they seem to be doing exceedingly well. From breakfast to lunch, their kitchen is serving up straight aces across the board—particularly, this quiche... that since my first bite has become my every daydream's constant companion. It has a texture that sets the bar for moist fluffiness, working synergistically with the seasonally inspired flavors to bring you on a stroll down savory lane... one forkful at a time.

> *Unfortunately, this page fails to have the capacity needed to romanticize their sweet creations justly— but go for the Bostock!*

Rise
The Stack

I tend to shy away from featuring eateries that haven't stood the test of time, simply because, they don't always last—and then you can't complete your Foodist Bucket List! However, while this breakfast spot is the new kid on the block, I'm confident that there potent combo of killer staff, unique ingredients (smoked brisket for breakfast? ...Yes, please!) creative dishes, and boozy drinks will secure them a longtime standing as a FoCo favorite! A beautiful display of their culinary work is this dish, which layers eggs, potatoes, and cheddar between slices of their homemade buttermilk biscuits—could it get any better? ...Only if you sat it on top of green chili, and added a slap of cilantro sour cream (check and check!).

Waltzing Kanagroo
Guinness Steak & Mushroom Pie

Americans' societal disinterest in the savory pies so adored by our "down under" friends has always puzzled me. I mean, we love food that can be eaten on the go and we love food that is delicious, yet for some reason we refuse to accept the self-contained flavor perfection that is savory pies. Anyway, when you decide you're ready to join the delicious #PiesDontHaveToBeSweetRevolution, meet me over at this joint! Owned by an Aussie couple, they serve up a variety of savory and sweet baked goodies, crafted in authentic Australian style. Of the hungry sort? Add a side of mushy peas and sweet potato mash to this signature pie for a bellyful of satisfying nourishment.

Maza Kabob
Aashak

You know the old saying, "Never judge an Afghan eatery by it's location"? Well those words of wisdom have never rung more true! This fast-casual style restaurant—situated in an unassuming strip mall—provides generous portions of lip-smacking authentic Middle Eastern dishes served alongside their routinely pleasant hospitality. While I'm keen on the sort of stomach satisfaction that comes from their various heaping piles of slow cooked meat, the uniqueness of this Afghan version of ravioli, with its assorted toppings and sauces, is a plated adventure in a class of its own.

Tip: *Their daily lunch specials* are on point.*
*Chicken korma and the kabobs! #Drool

Café De Bangkok
Northern Style Curry Noddle

According to archeological findings, turmeric, garlic, and ginger have been used as a dynamic culinary trio for at least 4,000 years. This makes curry the longest, continually produced dish that we know of... and as soon as you dig into this bowl, you'll know why. The best part of curry is its flexibility, affording every kitchen the chance to coax out their own style by tweaking the flavors and combining any number of unique add-ins. These guys take it sweet and savory with slow-cooked pieces of chicken in a rich coconut broth that is selfless with its bounty of spiced aromatics and flavor... and the "crunchies" on top make it that much better. Pro tip: Wash it down with a few gulps of their sip-it-straight-out-of-the-coconut water!

Austin's
Rotisserie Chicken

Dear Rotisserie Person at Austin's,

It is with great remorse that I write you this letter in regards to the indulgent piece of chicken that I had the privilege of devouring like a savage at your eatery last week. I would like to sincerely apologize for yelling like a banshee after taking my first bite, and for the chandelier that I broke with my final-bite-fist-pump. You see, my entire eating life has been a stumble from one flavorless chicken dish to another, always assuming that the best of poultry was the sauce it was smothered in. So you'll have to understand the ecstasy-like state that I transcended into with the first mouthful of your crisp-skinned, juicily tender, masterpiece.

Your biggest admirer,
Iver Marjerison

Tortillas Las 4 Americas
Sack of Fresh Tortillas

A fat sack of homemade 100% corn tortillas made daily and sold warm… for $2.50.

If that wasn't enough to make you drop what you're doing in reckless pursuit of this treasure… then we're not friends anymore.

Petra Grill
Lamb Kabob

Maybe it's some sort of primal trigger, buried deep in our DNA, that makes our stomachs yearn and puts the barbaric feeling of hunger on our mind as soon as kabobs are mentioned. After all, on its own it seems a bit culinarily lacking... surely it can't pack the flavor of a braise or sauté; it's just meat on a stick... how remarkable could it really be? Good question, and in the case of these particular meat-wrapped sticks of savory perfection... the answer is very, deeply, significantly, expressively, distinctly, unambiguously, monumentally... remarkable!

 # Star of India
Butter Chicken

"Dark" meat gets a bad wrap... it's not as lean, it can be tough... blah blah blah. Reality is, there are only two kinds of people in the world: those who love dark meat, and those who have never had it prepared properly. On the topic of preparation, this place's method of cooking it low and slow (to yield a wondrously soft texture) in a creamy tomato curry until the deep flavors exquisitely meld... A++. Beyond this dish, this restaurant is a true cornucopia, with an array of authentic Indian desserts, drinks, and eats sure to satisfy both veggie and meat lovers. We're talking: 13 different kinds of naan bread (go for the paneer-stuffed!), traditional chai tea, mango Lassi, and Gulab Jamun (Indian style donuts). It's an upscale-ish spot for dinner, and the price reflects that—but if you're looking to be economic, the lunch buffet is on point!

Don't forget a handful of toasted fennel on your way out the door!

DGT
The Bandito

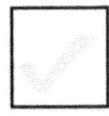

My scoring method for tacos revolves around the idea that the best are a celebration of masterfully crafted meat, and that its additional components are simplistic—purposed to augment the meat... not hide it's questionable texture or lacking flavor. With that being said, this taco—with it's overnight-cooked unimaginably tender pork, scallion salsa, and corn tortilla (ask for it)—on a scale of zebra to fifteen... is at least a solid red. And while they don't fall into as precise of a scoring methodology, I gotta say the quesadilla chips, breakfast bombshell, and cheese taco—with crisp cheese bits—are of near-equivalent awesomeness.

Pickle Barrel
The Balboa
...with AuJus*

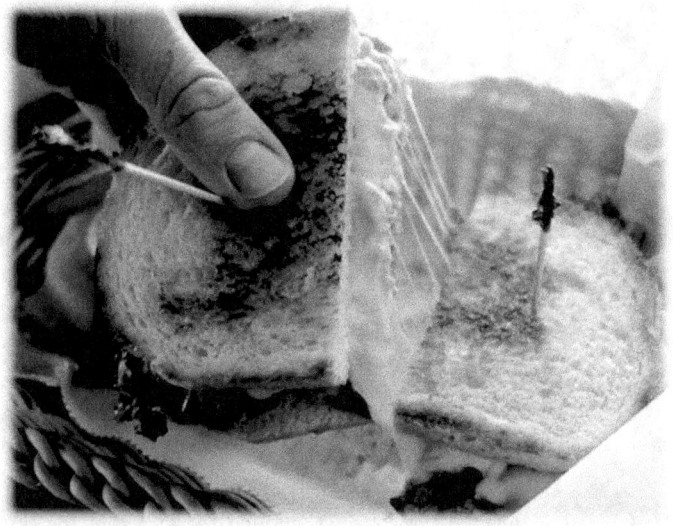

They say that artwork mirrors its creator, and that in the finest pieces, the viewer is actually able to catch a glimpse of the soul of the artist within the work. What then, can one gather about the soul of the artist behind this immaculate creation of garlic butter grilled roast beef, lavished with gooey mozzarella, gently piled between slices of perfectly toasted sourdough? One can only assume that the man behind such beauty is of the highest regards in culinary wisdom and flavorful nobility.

**Sub for the included marinara sauce,
and treat it like a French dip.*

FoCo Café
Community-Centric Lunch

In a heroic redefining of community, this volunteer-run non-profit café serves up nutritiously delicious food—largely donated from local restaurants and farms—lunch-line style*. Based on their mission to offer quality meals to all community members, all food is "pay what you can," and if you can't pay—you're welcome to volunteer instead. In tune with making the world a better place, their outdoor "Freedge" allows locals to leave/take excess produce in an attempt to reduce food waste... how cool is that?!

*Don't let this concept mislead you, the quality and flavors of the food have consistently proven to blow my hair back.

 Totally 80's Pizza
Awesome Frito Pie

Boasting to be the world's only 1980's museum, this one of a kind strip mall pizzeria has its walls covered in '80s memorabilia, including dozens of celebrity autographs, a six-foot carbonite Han Solo, a replica of Pee-Wee Herman's bicycle, and a life-size Terminator. As for the pizza—I'm going to be perfectly honest with you—with a dining experience this unique; they were gunna make the book regardless of food quality. With that being said, this pie is surprisingly bangin' good! Sure, the Frito chips, sour cream "drizzle," and optional 22k gold flake topping may seem a bit juvenile and bizarre, but I gotta say, devouring it under the knowing gaze of life-size Michael Jackson is an edible experience I wouldn't trade for two tickets to the Golden Spurtle.

Café Bluebird
Kentucky Corn Bread

Game Changer *[gay(m) chain·ger] noun*
1. *an event, idea, or procedure that effects a significant shift in the current manner of doing or thinking about something. [Oxford Dictionary]*

I had to get technical for this item, because I wanted to make it clear what exactly this dish has done... changed the breakfast game forever. Through an unprecedented combination of creative serendipity and culinary genius, this dish has singlehandedly dethroned the biscuit from its long stood position as gravy's best friend, deliciously replacing it with sweet homemade cornbread. The resulting mountain of hearty flavor has become my uncontested go-to for a stick-to-your-ribs breakfast.

Doug's Day Diner
Black Betty Burger

<u>Consciousness of</u>: Iver J. Marjerison
<u>Day on earth</u>: 9,261
<u>Location</u>: Milky Way

The smell of fresh green chilies, blackberry jam, peanut butter, and sharp cheddar permeate my consciousness. My eyes open, and I look down to the source of the rapturous aroma, a fat stack of what can only be called a burger sits in front of me. My eyes begin darting across the creation: admiring the immense patty, taking stock of the lavish adornments—omg, that really was the smell of PB&J!—and lusting over the oh-so-fluffy bread. Sounds, which can only be described as happiness, ring all around me, and my wandering gaze catches neighboring plates boasting generous portions of from scratch Tex-Mex inspired breakfast perfections…

Ginger & Baker
Brunch

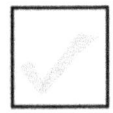

This is one of those places that just does one thing REALLY well. I mean sure, the cafe's bloody marys are perfect, and yes, they also have an awesome steakhouse, and of course, they do teach kombucha-making, among other classes, and I do want to eat everything in the bakery, and... okay, so I love a ton of stuff they do, but my point is — I LOVE love their brunch. :)

☑ Avogadro's Number
Tempeh Burger

Tempeh:
A traditional soy product originating from Indonesia. It is made by a natural culturing and controlled fermentation process that binds soybeans into a cake form. - Wikipedia

...So despite its bizarrely unappetizing description, this stuff is actually pretty good. Well actually, to be honest, most times I've had it... it's not that good—BUT, this place is different! Their homemade tempeh patties have an oddly irresistible texture of savory deliciousness, which is complemented splendidly by thick cuts of melted cheese and basic toppings, all of which is brought in sync with a rustic wheat bun... A noshing experience that lends itself perfectly to their brilliantly inclusive bar, open mic, live music, and various other events!

Big City Burrito
Potato Burrito

Each venture into this unassuming burrito joint is like a full-blown assault on all 5 senses. First, smell, as your nose catches flirting whiffs of the peppers being roasted; then, sight as your eyes become fixated on the 7-dozen hot sauce choices; followed by hearing, as you become slowly hypnotized by the meditative sounds of veggies being chopped and beans being boiled. After a brief back-and-forth with the burrito-monger—opting, of course, for the obligatory queso—touch finally gets its turn, as you wrap your hands around the gloriously warm burrito, reserving a brief moment of silence to appreciate its generous stuffing. All of this, climaxed by taste, as you bite through the alternating layers of crunchy fried potato, gooey queso, and smoky salsa... a total and complete sensory overload, in the most delicious sort of way.

The Crown Pub
Pommes Frites

Question: *What is the most consumed vegetable in the United States?*
Answer: *The potato*

This acclaimed status is thanks to, of course, the ingenious French fry, the humble side dish that has become nearly synonymous with the American meal. Unfortunately, this popularity has given way to uniformity, and really, they all taste the same: crispy and delicious. But amidst this sea of clones, one basket has risen above, securing a place in my mental realm reserved for all that is right in the world. At first I thought it was their delicately thin crispiness, or the traditional English pub atmosphere, and then I realized that what really set this fry experience apart, is that instead of having each bite drowned in the salty sweetness of crushed tomatoes, the fries are able to take center stage, complemented subtly by an exotic range of homemade sauces—personal favorite being the yellow curry. garlic truffle aioli).

Jax Fish House
Oyster Hour

Since serendipitously stumbling upon this daily ritual, I've awoken nightly with the same nightmare: I'm in a blurred eatery. I keep asking the waiter for the one-dollar oysters, but the waitress just keeps shaking her head while the entire restaurant heinously laughs at my request, as if it's the most absurd thing they've ever heard. I wake up in a cold sweat, and the feeling of an incomplete reality doesn't leave me until I'm back at Jax, once again shooting one-dollar oysters in a dreamlike bliss.

Krazy Karl's
Spicy Ranch

Disclaimer: *For logistical, financial, and serendipitous reasons, the author of this book was formerly a multi-weekend night patron of this once hole-in-the-wall pizza joint. The resulting bias is likely to be overt, obnoxious, and trump any logical contradictions.*

Want me to write you a poem romanticizing the chicken club grinder? Easy. Want me to make their pizza the topic of a motivational speech for the heroic zookeepers who have to deal with the juvenile antics of panda bears*? Done. Just know that at the heart of it all, it's not about the reasonable prices, the assault of flavor, or the impeccable crust... it's about the spicy ranch.

...it always has been—and always will be—about the spicy ranch.

*If you didn't understand this, YouTube "Panda messing with zoo keeper" asap.

Mt. Everest Café
Chicken MoMo

To the untrained eye, this may just seem like a haphazardly fried plate of "pot stickers"... but even to the untrained taste bud, the first bite will quickly prove otherwise. This particular style of dumpling—native to Tibet and Nepal—is made true-to-tradition, with the chicken spicing session being given as much attention as the from-scratch achar dipping sauce. As someone who takes your stomach's best interest very seriously, I'll have to suggest you pair these with a glass of the yogurt drink lassi, and make a point of carving adequate time out of your schedule to wreck their lunch buffet at least tri-weekly.

Slyce Pizza Co.
Mac & Cheese Pizza

Imagine if the un-matched savory-gooeyness of cheese, were to marry the nearly-perfect fold-and-nosh-ability of New York style pizza, and they were to have a kid who grew up and got his PhD in Quantum Childhood Nostalgia... that kid, would be this perfectly oversized slice of pizza.

Also, though I couldn't find a way to efficiently metaphoricalize it, they conveniently offer by-the-slice options, the staff is always friendly, the whole menu is quite affordable... and they have beer.

Back Porch Café
Huevos Rancheros

Breakfast Happiness Recipe:
1. *Start with one Mediterranean-style building.*
   (Preferably ~100 years old and off the beaten path)
2. *Add one oversized patio.*
   (Preferably surrounded by rustic greenery)
3. *Add a kitchen that smokes their own meat, makes chorizo, bakes fresh sourdough, and takes pride in their chili recipe.*
4. *Add a dish that stuffs a grilled jalapeño tortilla with beans and cheese, tops it with eggs, and smothers it in green chili.*
5. *Indulge.*

   For enhanced jubilation, I always suggest adding good company, a sunny day, and too much coffee.

The Colorado Room
Bison Poutine

You know that one friend, who—for lack of better words—is a little rough around the edges? You know the one; he makes crude jokes, prefers plot-less movies with lots of explosions, and speeds for the sake of speeding... Yet, despite his shortcomings, he's the first to have your back in a fight, tears up during the national anthem, and always cheers for the home team. Poutine* is kinda like that friend: you're a bit confused by him... but at the end of the day, he's the first person you call when you're looking for a good time.

*For those of you looking for information beyond irrelevant metaphors, poutine is a Canadian dish that covers French fries with gravy, cheese curds, and—in this case—slow cooked bison meat. This open-late eatery makes the best (maybe the only?) in town, and their high-energy atmosphere is perfect for enjoying board games, live music, and adult beverages.

William Oliver's
Pint-o-Bacon
...with a shot of maple syrup

Umami = "Pleasant savory taste"

It is one of the five basic tastes (along with sweetness, sourness, bitterness, and saltiness). Often described as "meaty," this flavor is most noted in foods rich in the amino acid glutamate—which unscientifically speaking—represent the majority of delicious things, including: cured meats, tomato sauce, hard cheeses, and soy sauce. Perhaps most notable, is the flavor's rich "umami bomb"-like presence in bacon.

Point being, the reason bacon is awesome? Science.

The reason this restaurant is awesome? Because they proudly rock a bacon-centric menu! ...Though the weekend DIY Bloody Mary and cereal bars certainly aren't hurting their awesome-score.

Nick's Burger & Brew Special

To-Do List:

- Drop socks at dry cleaner
- Learn to ukulele Jason Mraz's "I'm Yours"
- Add Twinkies to bug-out bag
- Finish FoCo Foodist book
- YouTube and master the "3 move checkmate"
- Find the best beer and burger deal in FoCo

This Colorado grass-fed burger—cooked to order with the perfect amount of "special sauce" and aged cheddar—is served with a pile of parmesan fries, homemade ranch, and a beer, for $10 every Tuesday.

Surfside 7
Wild Boar Corn Dog

Bars like this are usually known for the simple things: bargain beer, premixed shot specials, live music, and good times... but to earn local-love in a town like Fort Collins, you also have to have something rockin' in the kitchen. In this case, it's a hand dipped corn dog, made with "locally sourced" (still a bit confused about the logistics of this? But tasty nonetheless!) wild boar sausage. If you're asking, I suggest grabbing your stick after 7 o'clock to coincide with the nightly drink specials and checking their social media beforehand to ensure you have some live music while you sip and nosh.

Taqueria Delicias
Tacos y Tacos
...y Tacos y Tacos!

"Is there a lot of good Mexican food in Fort Collins?"

If by "Mexican food" you mean "tacos and burritos" ...then the answer is yes! With my taco-must-try-list already being too long, I really had no interest in adding another spot. That is, until this tortilla-laden perfection touched my lips. Let's put it this way: there are good tacos, there are utility tacos, and then there are these Tacos. Ones that encapsulate an entire cuisine within the borders of their tiny tortiallas, simutaniously bursting with flavor, while tantalizing your tastebuds with the nuances of ingredients that have been pain-stakeingly coaxed to the edge of perfection.

Note: *Not super Google-able. Though it is a food truck, it can generally be found at: 1311 N College Ave.*

Saigon Grill
Pho

Despite radical global differences, there is one common thread woven throughout the fabric of human eating... soup. This is for several reasons; most importantly, the process of slowly boiling foods is a method of drawing out otherwise inaccessible nourishment—as is the case with boiling bones to make a rich stock or broth. Secondly, the flavors drawn out... are delicious! Now in case you didn't know, a good soup isn't about what's floating in it—it's about the liquid. The problem is that in an industrialized effort to make food cheap, our broths have slowly become little more than over-salted water—likely responsible for our ubiquitous disinterest in soup. The good news is, as of recent, a properly prepared broth revolution is underway—with this Vietnamese noodle soup, and its flavorful assault of umami-bomb broth, leading the charge!

Hog Wild BBQ
Ribs

Want to know the secret to great tasting meat? It's not the cut, it's not the sauce, it's not the marinade, and it's not the deep fryer... the true secret is the ridiculously succulent fork-tender perfection that comes from cooking it low and slow. It sounds simple... and it is. The problem is this method creates a variety of logistical issues for restaurants; so most (even BBQ joints) opt for faster and easier methods—but not this joint! Owner Chris Robinson refuses to compromise, barbecuing his meat the old-fashioned way—beautifully low, and perfectly slow—over the heat of actual burning wood. Their variety of meats and sides (lunch platters offered for $10ish) are all selfless with flavor, but the indulgently tender pork ribs, shot through with savory smokiness, is my go-to's go-to.

Los Tarascos
Menudo

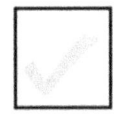

The correlation between prosperity and food is a funny thing. For example, as America increased in affluence, we began opting for foods that are deemed more prestigious—such as prime cuts of beef, chicken breasts, and tuna steaks. However, while these foods are more prestigious in the sense that they cost more, they are not necessarily any better when it comes to flavor. In fact, the richest flavors often come from the things that most Americans downright avoid, such as: bones, necks, feet, tails, heads, and.... organs. The most unfortunate result of this counter-intuitive eating trend is that it tends to be extremely wasteful. The second most unfortunate result is we miss out on a ton of rich, nostril-widening aromatics and palate-wakening flavors. Case in point: this traditional Mexican soup made of cow stomach. This joint prepares an exquisitely flavorful bowl, served only on weekends—which is perfect, as folklore claims the dish to be the ultimate cure for a hangover.

The Twisted Noodle
Loaded Garlic Bread

Gaining massive popularity in the last few years, the "fast casual" restaurant concept has established itself as an integral part of local food scenes. Problem is, it's not easy. Doing it properly requires maintaining a highly volatile juggle between quality, efficiency, and price point—a juggle that the family who owns this spot, does perfectly. The staff is efficient and friendly, the Italian dishes—which you would comfortably pay top dollar for at a white table cloth joint—are thoughtful and tasty, and the price point will make your wallet smile from crease to fold (i.e. their daily special loaded GB for <$3.00).

Lyric Cinema Café
Cereal Bar
...and Cartoons!

If there is a better way to spend a weekend morning than overindulging in an all-you-can-eat cereal bar as you watch your favorite cartoons on the big screen... you'll have to let me know, because I personally, have yet to find anything that comes close. So, you ask, what particular strain of genius is responsible for creating such a perfect embodiment of bliss-filled childhood nostalgia? The same kind responsible for creating a locally adored indie theater with bargain ticket prices, beer and wine, boba tea, and real food.

Fiona's Delicatessen
Tara Lee's
A True Honey

With homemade baked goods and pastries, scores of novel salad and sandwich creations, a '70s style milkshake bar, and even a half-dozen different hot dog options, this place is great for people who... well, actually? It's great for just about anyone! From veggie lovers to dedicated carnivores, those sweet-tooth inclined and those just looking for an on-the-go snack, the old-school atmosphere combined with a deliciously new age take on ingredient combinations has something that will leave just about anyone's stomach nodding with satisfaction—especially if you're into absurdly fluffy and moist homemade banana bread, smeared thick with creamy peanut butter, drizzled with Colorado honey, and generously laden with toasted almonds... yeah, it's safe to say that if you're into that sort of thing, your going to love this place!

JeJu
Chicken Bi-Bi-Go
(Bibimbop)

If you were to directly translate this Korean word, you would find that its literal meaning—mixed rice bowl—paints a grossly oversimplified image of this dish. Well, actually, it is fairly simple... essentially, it's just sautéed and exotically seasoned veggies with chicken (or beef or tofu), and gouchujang sauce—which combines the umami-laden greatness of fermented soy with the spiced kick of chili peppers—over top of a bed of rice, topped with a fried egg, and served sizzling on a hot stone. However, while the ingredient list is seemingly simple, after you sauce and toss, the bowl transforms into a mouth watering mosh pit of flavors so gripping that you end up questioning the meaning behind any dish that differs... or at least any meal that doesn't come with gouchujang sauce.

Sally's Kitchen
Ginger Avodaco Fried Rice

If you were to judge this humble gas station kitchen by it's cover you'd probably make some assumptions... and in terms of the deep-fried items, dish presentation, and other Chinese food assumptions—for the most part—you'd be right. BUT what you'd be wrong about is the tender loving care and creativity that Sally puts into many of her signature dishes, like this pile-o-nom! For $10-ish you can get a heaping mound of fried rice (easily split between two people), mixed with shrimp, beef, and chicken, with so much don't-have-to-ask-or-pay-more-for avocado that Qdoba is put to shame... and more spicy ginger-ness than you could throw a Pringle at!

Jim's Wings
RamHot Wings

Food Facts:

1. *Ketchup originated as a fermented fish sauce in Asia ...containing zero tomatoes.*
2. *The fear of cooking is known as mageirocophobia.*
3. *These fiery hot wings, paired with a pitcher and good friends... is the best thing that has ever happened to me.*
4. *Despite the "crème filling"... Oreos do not contain dairy.*

Taqueria Los Comales
Offal-Taco-Trio

This epic taco feast consists of barbacoa (beef cheeks), lengua (beef tongue), and tripa y buche (beef and pork stomach), traditionally prepared to ensure an explosion of tender flavor that quickly has you forgetting the offbeat origins of the fillings. These tacos are served on authentic corn tortillas, with nothing forced upon you but a pinch of cilantro and onions... from there, you're in the flavor-driver-seat, steering the experience any direction you like with their elaborately stocked salsa bar—which includes whole roasted jalapeños! Pair with one of their homemade drinks—lemonade, horchata, or cantaloupe juice (personal favorite)—and you're in for a Mexican meal of time-honored epicness.

*Unofficial name that I created. "Offal" is a culinary term that refers to the organs of an animal. It's not a Spanish word, and does not appear on their menu. These tacos need to be ordered individually.

Charco Broiler
The Pepper Bob

No socially engaging online presence, no fancy menu wording, and no foodies taking photos of their food... dining at this no-frills family owned restaurant is exactly what you would expect: the service is we-know-each-other-even-if-we-don't sort of friendly, they serve staple American fare, the butter is served generously, the atmosphere defines homey, and it's almost obligatory to finish things off with a slice of pie and coffee. In fact, there is really only one thing surprising about this place... how creative they get with their steaks! Case in point, this innovative six-ounce sirloin that's heavily pepper-marinated for two days before being broiled on a skewer. The result? A tender flavor festival of peppery perfection!

II: Drinks

*From boozy to nourishing,
a compilation of all things sipped*

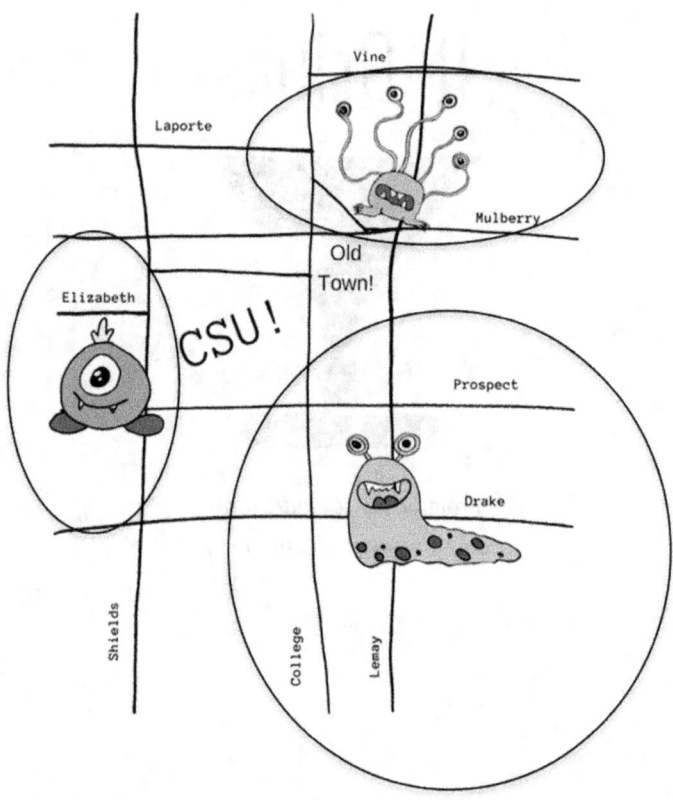

I decided to hand make the map to give it a "treasure hunt" feel (also because I couldn't figure out the legal logistics of printing Google Maps). In case it's not clear, the monsters represent the region of their adjacent list of breweries.

Fort Collins
Breweries!

- O New Belgium Brewing Company
- O Pateros Creek Brewing Company
- O Coopersmith's Pub & Brewing
- O Odell Brewing Company
- O Fort Collins Brewery
- O Equinox Brewing
- O Horse & Dragon Brewing Company
- O Snowbank Brewing
  Funkwerks Inc.

- O Three Four Beer Co.
- O CB & Potts Brewery
- O Ramskellar Pub
- O Intersect Brewing
- O McClellan's Brewing
- O _____

- O Jessup Farm Barrel House
- O Black Bottle Brewery
- O Rally King Brewing
- O Maxline Brewing
- O Zwei Brewing
- O Gilded Goat Brewing Company
  _____

Bean Cycle Roasters
The Kerouac

Shelves full of books, fast WiFi, comfortable seats, juice bar, and bomb coffee... I mean, isn't that enough to get you here? Fine... how about a confusingly romantic poem for this beloved drink?

> *With years of courting only coffees hot and bold,*
> *I believed that nothing else I would ever hold,*
> *Then one day I crossed a cold brewed mug,*
> *It's Venetian crème perfection I had to chug,*
> *Since it's touched my lips, I can never look back,*
> *Forever mine, in the name of caffeine, my dear Kerouac.*

Social
Traditional Absinthe Service

You descend the stairs into this underground fantasy, and almost immediately the powerful ambiance engulfs you, transporting you to a distant land... a magical place where things like flamed oranges, short bread cookies, and saffron have a place in mixed drinks. A place where smoked tea can become a part of your cocktail experience, where Chartreuse—the preferred drink of the Great Gatsby himself—pours frequently, and a place where you can finally experience the traditional serving method of the infamous Absinthe, a mystical spirit long celebrated for its (arguably fictitious) psychoactive properties.

Did I mention the incredible selection of meat and cheese boards, and actually-unbelievable happy hour prices? **This is <u>the</u> place for cocktails in FoCo.**

UNION Bar & Soda Fountain
"White Lightning" Spirited Shake

"Spirited Floats" and "Fortified Shakes"

...Crafted purposefully, and delciously, in a high-energy atmosphere with great food and proffesional service—awesome—obviously. But what else would you expect from the team behind the boozie-perfection that is Social (#59)? This shake is my go-to, employing the flavor magic of burbon, carmel, and sea salt. But if you're feeling nostalgic, shoot for the Roots & Herbs—a sophisticated take on your classic rootbeer float.

Ramskeller Pub
Ram Brew

Housed in the Lory Student Center, this spot has served as an invaluable spot for students and faculty to relax, converse, and work since 1968. Along with the pool tables and live entertainment offerings, they boast a variety of pub fare and drinks... including 20 beers on tap. While it's unique enough to have a beer-serving haven in the student center, what really sets it apart is the attached microbrewery, which will provide Rams and the general public with the unique opportunity to sip on whatever the Fermentation Science and Technology* students have been experimenting with!

*Yes, this is a full B.S. degree. Yes, it could set you on track to become a brewmaster. Yes, it is awesome.

Harbinger Coffee
The Single Origin Pour Over

The average person might call Jonathan Jarrow's enthusiastic dedication to crafting the perfect cup of coffee something like... "obsessive". But personally I find that word to be a grossly juvenile understatement, far from properly capturing the elite level of raw dedication that he has put into honing his craft. This unparalleled passion manifests at his laboratory-like coffee shop, where his team of equally passionate baristas use digital scales, thermometers, and space-age-looking equipment to meticulously craft each cup, ensuring maximum extraction of the coffee bean's most delicate flavors and aromatics.

Go for the pour over style, choose the origin of your bean, and enjoy the show!

Gelato & aMore
Hazelnut Gelato

Scientifically-speaking: *gelato differs from traditional ice cream largely in terms of its fat, with gelato using a higher portion of whole milk and less cream, giving it a fat content around 5% (ice cream in the US must legally be a minimum of 10%). However, despite its lower fat content, proper gelato offers a mouthfeel that often seems even richer than its creamed counterpart. This is larger due to the slower speed that gelato is churned at, which whips less air into the mixture, making it denser. Also contributing to its unique texture, is the fact that gelato is often served at a slightly warmer temperature.*

Not-scientifically-speaking: *these scoops are darned delicious.*

(Also! They have incredible vegan sorbet.)

Old Elk Distillery
Peanut Butter Whiskey

Photo: Corbin Parker

Mexico has tequila, Scotland has scotch, France has Champagne, and America... has bourbon! These liquids define their land of origin, embody the culture, and, fun fact, legally can't be made anywhere else! This distillery takes its American Heritage seriously, and approaches its whiskey-making with pride, resulting in a flagship bourbon that has the taste of passion in every drop. They also have peanut butter whiskey, which is both silly and delicious! :)

Happy Lucky's Teahouse
3 Shades of Green

Whether you're looking for a simple tea-lent caffeine fix, or on the hunt for a knife to break up your pu-erh bricks in style... this is your spot! Now, like many Americans, I grew up perma-seeping bags of Lipton whenever I needed to smooth out a coffee binge or ward off colds. So I admit, the idea of treating three different green teas like they were Napa's finest reds seemed a bit silly. Fortunately—like with most things that matter—intuition failed me. With my first few sips, I found myself serendipitously caught in a rapturously profound tasting experience... with the subtle yet distinct flavors and aromas of each cup singing and dancing to its own special tune across my unsuspecting palate.

Pinball Jones
Pinball Beer

I invite you to take a few minutes out of your busy day, to construct a sort of hypothetical "check-list" compiling all of the things that really make you happy...

If your list has 2 or more of the following items, PJ's is the place for you! If not... you misunderstood the question.

<u>*Happiness*</u>
-Too many pinball machines
-All the best arcade games
-Free popcorn
-Craft beer

Ku Cha Tea
Full Matcha Service

Technically speaking, "matcha" is just green tea—or the dried leaves of the Camellia Sinensis tree. However, it differs slightly from more common versions in both cultivation and processing, with the biggest difference being that the leaves are ground into a fine powder that is dissolved—not steeped—in hot water. While this highly caffeinated powder is now found in the form of "pour-and-shake" drink mixes, this is a more traditional experience, using authentic tools and preparation methods to celebrate the ceremonial aspects that traditionally embodied this meditative drink.

Black Bottle Brewery
Cerealiously Count Chocula

Each sip of this full-bodied "Cereal Milk Stout" provides the sort of satisfying blast of nostalgia that can only come from a heavy load of —you guessed it! —Count Chocula cereal. What I love about this brew is the brewmaster's dedication to authenticity. Refusing to just add chocolate extract to a dark beer and slap it with a cool name, they went for the real deal! So how'd they do it? By literally buying out entire supplies of 'Chocula from local grocery stores.

Warning: this product is seasonal—so keep your eyes peeled!

Rocket Fizz
Bizarre Soda

People always ask, "Hey Iver, how can you be so sure that Old Town Fort Collins is the happiest place on earth?" Unfortunately, I have yet to find a way to accurately verbalize my admiration for this small slice of town, so I fall back on the facts, like it being the inspiration for Walt Disney's Main Street USA, the high ratio of dogs to humans, and the magnificence of its candy store—which in this case is an eclectic shop packed full of bizarre sodas, obscure candy, and happy people.

Rio Grande
Classic Rio Margarita

Iver Marjerison
@Iver_marjerison

HOLY SHMOKES ,,,Npw I know why thers a 3 marg limit!!1!1! @MyRioGrande

10:29 PM - 15 Dec 2016 from Fort Collins, CO

Warning: *The above Tweet is an act of hyperbolic expression. The author, publisher, and affiliated parties do not condone over-consumption of alcohol, public displays of intoxication, or incoherent social media usage.* <u>However</u>, *while the above tweet is not an accurate reflection of the author's margarita consumption, when he does indulge, he prefers the Thursday specials at this fine establishment... frequently paired with the chili rellenos.*

Mo Jeaux's
The Beaver

What do you get when you combine half a dozen different well liquors, grenadine, beer, sprite, and a whimsical assortment of other bar-liquids? Well, prior to my discoveration (how is that not a word?) of this college-friendly watering hole, I would have told you... a headache. Which, you may still find to be true; depending on how many friends you recruit to help you out! ...Whatever the case, I stand by the wise words of a stumbling undergrad: "You haven't finished FoCo, until you've finished The Beaver at Mo Jeaux's."

Lucky Joe's
Traditional Irish Coffee

*I once found myself wandering
Dublin with my worries the least.
As I spotted a café, I fancied a feast.
Now I knew it was early, but wanted to blend.
So I ordered a Bailey's and coffee…
as I knew was the trend.
As the red-bearded man laughed in my face,
I learned that was for the girls, and true Irishmen whiskeyed their coffee straight.
Since my return, I've long kept an eye peeled,
For an Irish bar that knows the real deal,
Alas! I found this peanut cluttered joint,
Where the Irish coffee is authentically on point.*

Trail Head Tavern
Iconic Dive Bar Beer

Dive Bar Must-Haves:

- ✓ *Cheap beer all the time*
- ✓ *Walls covered in marker*
- ✓ *Multiple pool tables*
- ✓ *Fiercely loyal group of local patrons*
- ✓ *"Meatloaf Monday"*

Town Pump
White Lightening & Toxic Fruit

If you're anything like me, your entire alcohol-consuming experience has been one big quest to find a bar where 'shine isn't some unknown liquor, exiled to collecting dust on a back rack, but instead is treated with the respect it deserves. The kind of place that celebrates "Moonshine Monday," that enthusiastically lists daily flavors on a chalkboard, and that is knowledgeable enough to know that moonshine pairs perfectly with only one thing... fruit soaked in Everclear. These innovative strides put these guys on the frontlines of the emerging moonshine movement. And before you erroneously mock the potential of this small bar to start a liquid revolution, remember, they were the first bar to serve Fat Tire.

Elliot's Martini Bar
Colorado Herb

Cocktails were originally a method of enhancing the liquor experience. Subtle flavors were added through bitters, liqueurs, herbs, and fruits, all meant to provide a mellow backdrop to augment the alcohols inherent taste. Overtime, this art of mixology has largely deteriorated, giving way to glasses of juice or soda meant to completely drown out alcohol's tune, enabling imbibers to drink recklessly while playing Russian-roulette with their blood sugar levels. Amidst this crazy world, Elliot's is a breath of fresh air, serving martinis that let the liquor take center stage, with the sharp edges smoothed out by artful and unique additions—in this case lemon, rosemary, and thyme.

They also serve a nut bowl that doesn't include peanuts... which I have an insane amount of respect for, and not because I'm allergic, but because those damn legumes have gotten away with their masqueradings for too long!

Feisty Spirits
Locally Distilled Whiskey Flight

In the midst of the local brewery craze, I've found many people don't realize that FoCo's craft alcohol scene also offers distilleries! Like this spot, where distiller/owner Jamie offers a range of traditional options, along with some unique stuff like quinoa whiskey, schnapps, and even a less-organ-bleaching version of Fireball! Located just out of the Old Town bustle, the tasting room is small and personal, the staff is always friendly, and the mood is always happy.

Sipping hard alcohol straight not your thing? No worries! They got a Peanut Butter Oreo Whiskey Milkshake that has your name written all over it.

Horse & Dragon
Sad Panda

Maybe it's the nowhere-else-I'd-rather-be patio…
Maybe it's the contagious positive energy
emitting from the employees…
Maybe it's this beer's ability to fulfill the robust flavor
of a coffee stout, without the often-accompanied syrupy sweetness…
Maybe head brewer Lindsey knows magic…
Or maybe it's just the cool name…

…But for whatever reason, this single item was suggested to me more than anything else during my research. Significantly more. I had hundreds of people tell me about it—literally. Try it for yourself, and I'm sure you'll see why.

The Whiskey
Whiskey Sour

- **1750-ish** — Sailors mix lemon/lime with diluted booze (likely in an attempt to combat scurvy and poor water quality).
- **1862** — Jerry Thomas' book, *The Bartenders Guide*, lists a recipe for the first "Whiskey Sour."
- **1880** — Egg whites become a common addition to the original recipe.
- **1920** — Prohibition Era (consumption of whiskey sours arguably increases).
- **1960** — Commercialized "sour mix" becomes a norm, replacing fresh lemons.
- **1990** — People realize actual lemons are awesome. Bartenders using fresh ingredients becomes emerging trend.
- **2016** — I TASTE WHISKEY SOUR PERFECTION!

THE WHISKEY SOUR TIMELINE

The Copper Muse Distillery
The Capone

A truly worthwhile Bloody Mary requires a potent combination of quality ingredients, innovative bartenders, and a creative passion for flavor. All of which, are why this place tops my charts with this featured Bloody rocking a mess of the usual suspects, combined with pickle juice and vodka that owner/distiller Jason crafts in the same building! Of their 50+ vodka (and rum) varieties and infusions, I've found the bacon and jalapeño to be the perfect augment to this spicy beverage.

The Fort Collins
Beer Immersion

Ask twenty different Fort Collinsanites (?) where to go to experience beer, and you'll get twenty-two different answers—and they will all be great. So while this is a curation of some personal favorites, I don't pretend that it's a full representation of the local beer scene; it is just one glorious way to immerse yourself in the brewing culture.

1. O'Dell Brewery patio—*Just up the street from New Belgium Brewery, this place is a true embodiment of a good time. Tons of outdoor seating, a music venue, food trucks, and happy people... I know of few better ways to spend a summer day.*

2. New Belgium Brewery tour—*a FoCo landmark, this brewery tour is educational, entertaining, and free! They book up fast, but if you don't make the list you can always hangout in their awesome taproom and wait for a no-show.*

3. Tap and Handle tasters—*70+ rotating taps and 120+ bottles; but the variety is what makes them my #1 beer bar, boasting seven different categories ranging from crisp and simple to "Tart and Funky". Go for at least one $2 glass from each category—sort of like a flight, except they don't use the term and look at me funny when I say it.*

4. Hops and Berries—*Once you've toured and tasted, the only thing left to do is get hands on! This home brew supply store makes it easy. They have all the supplies needed to craft your own beer/wine, and even teach classes—plus, their staff are insanely passionate, helpful, and happy to assist newbies.*

Scrumpy's Cider
Summit Flight

While the cider movement is slowly catching hold, progress seems to be hindered by the misconception that it's just another newfangled sugar-loaded replacement for non-beer drinkers (and gluten-avoiders). Reality is, years ago, the complex flavors and crisp drinkability of cider actually afforded it a top spot on America's alcohol totem. It was so popular, in fact, that it actually helped kick start an apple-tree planting rampage—and here you thought ol' Johnny was just in it for something to snack on! While many of today's pseudo-versions drink like a syrupy cousin of Mike's Hard, these guys are on a mission to help cider reclaim its celebrated status by hand crafting batches of subtle sweetness augmented by an exotic range of fruits (local crab apples!), herbs, and spices. Beyond this flight of their made-in-back offerings, they offer dozens of more varieties, all of which play nicely with their complimentary board games, live music, small plates, and positive energy.

Wilbur's Total Beverage
Wine Sampling

"...and from the red corner! Weighing in at the size a bloated super market, hailing from just off S College Ave., with a combined professional record of a million wins and zero losses, rated as one of the best pound-for-pound beer and wine retailers in Fort Collins, it's the infamous liquor store behemoth, the undisputed champion of the "bomber" section, holding a bazillion gold metals in customer service... the one, the only, Wilbur's Total Beverage of Fort Collins!"

While this tale of the tape is largely drawn from figments of my own imagination, this liquor store really is something remarkable. Beyond their unimaginable quantity of wine, beer, and spirits, what really sets them apart is the booze-knowledge and helpfulness of the staff... which is well represented with their free weekend wine tastings! (They do beer as well, but I figure #57 will keep you busy enough with local brews).

Blind Pig
$1 Mimosa

Sure, their mimosas are as strong as you'd expect a bargain drink to be, but I personally find the questionable Champagne ratio to be balanced out by their half-dozen different flavors and can't-be-beat prize tag*. Combine with their brunch buffet—which perfectly splits the difference between Caesar's Palace and the Holiday Inn—and you're fully equipped for a bountiful morning of drinking and eating at a price that reeks of reason.

*Many competing "bottomless" specials are priced $10-15. I've calculated this deal to be superior, as most places pour them equally strong, and most people don't drink more than a dozen.

Blue Agave
Margarita Flight

I'm the kind of guy that's always quick with confident-yet-uninformed advice: I can tell you the best knot to keep your hedgehog from running away, the time of day based on cloud movement, or what kind of pool stick makes the best oar. But when it comes to choosing which Margarita to order... I'm utterly and painfully clueless. My entire life I've ordered one kind, only to find hateful thoughts of jealousy forming for my neighbor's differing flavor. So for obvious reasons... when I caught wind of this margarita flight, I had to find an excuse to write an entire book just to share it with the world!

Golden Poppy Herbal Apothecary
Personalized Tea Blend

"...Toss your own salad or eat with the masses from their narrow trough."
- Tom Robbins

Truly a choice we each face daily, with an industrialized food system that has been curated to meet the desires of the masses. The problem with this formula is that it ignores individual preferences, with its sole purpose being to create stuff that everyone will like... and little attention given to what one person might love. It's sorta like playing darts with mashed potatoes; you hit the board, but rarely land a bull's-eye. With the increasing popularity of this formula, the personalized style that this place takes is truly a breath of fresh air! With hundreds of different herbs, roots, and organics to choose from, their experts will help you formulate your own blend to perfectly suit your health, allergy, or flavor needs.

Cooper Smith's
Sigda's Green Chili Golden Ale

As the world becomes oversaturated with new beers, microbrewers old and young have turned toward bizarre ingredients to make their batches stand out. Unfortunately, these sensational attention-seeking stunts often result in good stories and bad beer—which I had erroneously assumed to be the case with this particular ale. Naturally, I was starstruck upon my first sip, finding that the spiced intensity of the Anaheim and Serrano chilies—rather than overpower or clash with the crisp notes of the ale—actually complemented its subtle malty-sweetness. This unlikely flavor union has created a refreshingly novel brew that left my taste buds—though admittedly a bit confused—pleased and yearning.

III: Desserts

*Bizarre to traditional…
the who's who of the local sweet scene*

Nuance
Single Origin Taster Flight

"Terroir" *refers to the set of natural environmental factors that affect the characteristics of a food crop, such as climate and soil.*

You may be skeptical of terroir's impact on the taste of food—I mean, are grapes from Napa really that much better?—but this chocolate shop might convince you otherwise. Each of the 5 bars that you sample are made in house from full cacao beans, each sourced from a different part of the world. In total, they craft about 20 single origin chocolates, giving them the largest selection in the world. As you taste through your flight, what do you pick up? A hint of plums perhaps? Leather? Charred oak? A bit of coffee? Remember, there is nothing but sugar and cacao in these bars, so those complex aromas and flavors? ...That's the power of terroir!

Copoco's Honey
Orange Cinnamon Creamed Honey

It's a complex question, with no simple answer, but if you ever find yourself wondering if a particular town is a worthwhile destination for edible adventures, just ask yourself, "Is there a honey store?" In this case, the answer is yes! Complete with all sorts of beekeeping supplies, Colorado-sourced honey, tasty treats—like homemade baklava!—and this somehow-not-internationally-renowned Orange Cinnamon Creamed Honey. While an afternoon spent sampling the different varieties (maple honey anyone?!) is obviously a time, the real adventure is getting hands on with one of their beekeeping classes!

 # Walrus Ice Cream
Joke Flavor

Lisa and her team of ice cream-crafting rock stars have got to be some of my favorite people in the Western Hemisphere. They scoop generously, create locally inspired flavors, let you mix and match their 29-ish 'creams at will, and—best of all—they make a weekly "joke flavor." I'm talking: Mac n' Cheese, McDonald's Happy Meal, and the infamous "Blueberry Taco." All right, I confess, the joke flavor is only given as a free sample… so the cone in the picture? A perfect stack of Jackchip (made with Jack Daniel's!), butter pecan, and Swiss dark chocolate!

Vern's Toffee House
Best-You-Eva-Had Almond Toffee

While I hate to be a pessimist, it's my humble opinion, that many modern methods of food cultivation and preperation tend to prize low-costs above flavor and quality. From those lifeless red balls that the grocery store calls tomatoes, to mold-proof super breads loaded with more sugar then grain, there is a battle being waged, and many of our favorite foods have suffered. Luckily for Fort Collins, we have Vern's. This family run shop has been making toffee the good ol' fashion way, and putting a metaphorical middle-finger in the face of newfangled shortcuts since 1976! None of that cheap cornsyrup-thickened rapeseed oil nonsense that you can't keep from sticking in your teeth... no sir, this toffee here? Is the real deal.

Rainbow Café
Pumpkin Bread French Toast

What exactly puts this French toast so above-and-beyond awesome? That's hard to say... could it simply be their baked-in-house pumpkin bread? Or maybe it's the delicate sweetness of the grilled bananas? Or, perhaps, it's the satisfying textural combo of crunchy walnuts and velvety whipped cream? ...Then again, maybe it's just the generous pour of butter rum sauce?

Anyway... I give up. If you figure it out, let me know!

La Creperie & French Bakery
Perfectly Plain Croissant

Basically, the things in life that matter can be separated into two categories: food (Oreos and camel steaks), and art (chalk drawings and banjo strumming). But then, there's this gray area... full of the items that seem to simultaneously inhabit both of these majestic realms. Prime example... this authentic French café and bakery's indulgent croissant, masterfully crafted at the skillful hand of a true Frenchman, its perfect lamination shot through with infinite layers of buttery, airy perfection. Add in the fact that they import their butter from Europe and let their dough undergo a slow, traditional fermentation process, and what you have is nothing short of a masterpiece.

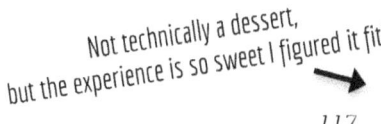

Not technically a dessert, but the experience is so sweet I figured it fit!

Café Vino
Toffee Date Cake

As a rule of thumb, when it comes to the food and beverage world, you can do one thing great, or a lot of things decently. A good example of this is the 15-page menu at Denny's compared to your local fine dining establishment that may only serve 4 different cuts of steak. This eatery, however, is the exception to this rule... because they knock it out of the park from breakfast (Huevos!) to dinner, and take it further with their drinks (wine flights!) and tapas menu that make them a choice spot to sip and converse. Despite their aces across the board, this must-try was still a shoe in: warm toffee sauce drizzled over homemade date cake, with an enticing ball of fig newton ice cream.

Alley Cat Coffee House
Chai Milkshake

~~This~~ 24 hour coffee house ~~boasts an impressive array of drinks and food alike, with lots of seating and lounging area, making it a hangout for college kids. The real star is their~~ made-in-house chai ~~that makes for delicate as hot or cold drink, and packs the sort of spices that you've never got from the more commercial stuff. A chai shake, which became popular.~~

The empty glass speaks for itself.

Cheeba Hut
Cereal Bars

After spending any amount of time in Colorado, this iconic sandwich shop is sure to bubble to the surface of a conversation or two. Their unapologetic ~~acceptance~~ celebration of Colorado's "green" culture manifests itself in sandwiches named after cannabis strains, and size choices that range from "nugs" to "blunts." But don't be fooled, their fame isn't just due to sensationalism! They rock a variety of I'd-come-back-again sandwiches (Durban Diesel #ftw), and other unique "munchies" …of distinct edible brilliance however, are these beautifully simple bliss balls of finger-licking nostalgia.

Butter Cream Cupcakery
Mini Cupcakes

You know those special socks you have? You slip them on, and no matter what the world throws at you, you know, that everything will be okay. It becomes as if the sun is serving up your own special brand of warmth... and every moment your feet spend snuggly wrapped in their cloth embrace is the right moment.

...Well, an afternoon spent noshing your way through a handful of this spot's 60 rotating cupcake flavors is sort of like that! ...Except the feet stuff—your feet are likely to feel mediocre at best.

Lucile's Creole Café
Beignets

Cajun-food 101: *When French colonists living in Canada were kicked out of their homes in the 1700s, many of them relocated to Louisiana. This relocation created an unlikely marriage between the unique flavors and ingredients of the Gulf region and traditional French culinary techniques. This delicious merger gave way to an entirely new culture of food so delicious that 300 years later it is the inspiration behind one of Fort Collins' most coveted breakfast spots. With masterfully spiced and sauced dishes across the board, you really can't go wrong, just be sure to start or finish—or both—your dining session with one of these New Orleans-style doughnuts, perfectly fried and covered in enough powdered sugar to bury a hobbit.*

City Drug
European Goodies

Proudly serving Fort Collins for over 62 years, this family run pharmacy provides the ususal suspects of convience items, medical knick-knacks, and of course... "year-around" European goodies and treats! From preserves and baking supplies, to Dutch chocolate and and German candy. This wall of delicious offers a beautiful mix of classic favorites, and difficult-to-comprehend noveltieis.

Can't figure out the item in the photo? ...That's the point!

Mary's Mountain Cookies
Salted Caramel Cookie Ice Cream Sandwich
...with Chocolate Chip Cookie Dough Ice Cream!

Pie... candy corn... cake... all the usual desserts... are a lot like rock and roll. Their flavors are loud and they hit your taste buds fast and hard. The richness makes a lot of noise, and your mouth experiences a fast-and-sweet jam fest. A quality ice cream sandwich, on the other hand, is different; it's more like jazz. The delectable chewiness of freshly baked cookies taps a mellow harmony, while the richness of the generously scooped 'cream keeps a decisively subtle tempo. The lightweight rhythm that it sings to your taste buds is fluid and sensual; it draws lines, but sets no boundaries... certainty and wonder intertwine. It's the kind of dessert that makes you forget woes and ignore loved ones, as you slip into a sugary bliss.

Snooze
Pancake Flight

There really isn't much to say about this place... because honestly, the Saturday morning line that wraps around the block 19 times speaks for itself—but the page would look goofy if left blank, so here goes: This quaint eatery-turned multi-state breakfast mogul, is known for remastering traditional breakfast favorites (both eats and adult drinks!) with imaginatively delicious flare. Perhaps earning highest esteem, are their pancakes... that, fortunately for all of us, need not be limited to one flavor! And while the wait to be seated tends to be just long enough to rethink your entire life, don't worry... they provide free coffee. ☺

- Insider Tip #1: They let you sub one pancake, for one French toast.
- Insider Tip #2: Get the secret menu Cinnamon Roll French Toast.
- Insider Tip #1 for Insider Tip #2: Ask for it "sinful" (adds bacon!).

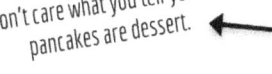

I don't care what you tell yourself, pancakes are dessert.

Starry Night
Cappucino Cake

Attention World:
This. Is. The. Cake.

I'm talking about coffee and cocoa flavors so immaculately intertwined that you consider licking it so you don't have to share. I'm talking about a crafting so gorgeous that it has your grandma reaching for her camera. The entire experience is a rapturous sensory eruption: the exhilarated anticipation as you order, the euphoric neurological overload as you eat it, and then—like a thief in the night—it's gone... and the residual bliss of spending time with this flawlessly moist slice of utopia leaves you rethinking your life, questioning your beliefs, and rewriting your dreams.

Revolution Artisan Pops
Cucumber Lime
Pop~~sicle~~

The word "popsicle," for better or for worse, is nearly synonymous with all that is juvenile, acting as a frozen manifestation of childhood innocence and helplessness... Which is why that word is not being used in this case. This "ice pop," while of similar resemblance, is a breed of it's own, boasting both sophistication and intellect at levels that the humble popsicle has never known. The sort of frozen treat that if you were to sketch a portrait of, would be wearing a top hat, carrying a cane, and gazing out from two very wise eyes. Handcrafted and organic, with locally sourced ingredients hailing from both #harbinger and #nuance, these refreshingly-not-overly-sweet treats, pack the sort of complex flavor punch that "popsicles" can only dream of attaining.

Churn
Space Junkie Cone

@Lorieatsicecream

I (along with every other warm-blooded human being who has ever had the privilege of eating their ice cream) am a big fan of Little Man Ice Cream in Denver. So naturally, when they opened up a location in FoCo, I sold all of my possessions and asked if I could rent the loft above their shop and eat their ice cream all day long. To my surprise, they said yes! I just can't live upstairs and I have to pay full price. :)

Ace Gillett's
Ganache Brownie

I figure you guys are getting sick of my opinion by now, so I'll let you take the reigns for this dish...

Live jazz, classy drinks, and _____ eats, the atmosphere of this basement lounge is the perfect combo of classy and casual (no dress code). While their team's professionalism and the live entertainment are enough to make a _____ consider _____, what has me _____ is this _____ dessert. The _____ richness of the chocolate brownie, wrapped up in crispy philo dough, is like _____ when the _____. To add to this splendor, rested atop, are scoops of homemade ice cream acting like _____ in search of _____... creating a _____ dessert experience.

 # Me Oh My Coffee & Pie
Seasonal Pie

Located just north of town, this unassuming roadside café is the workshop for some of the best homespun pies that Northern Colorado has to offer. Now, due to the seasonal nature of the menu, you never really know what will be available, but rest assured that whatever inspiration of the moment has caught master pie-crafter Caitlin's culinary imagination, is going to be fist-fight-over-the-last-bite status. But how can I be so sure that her creations are made from-scratch with tender loving care? Easy... I don't even need ice cream when I eat a slice of her apple pie.

DO NOT UNDER ANY CIRCUMSTANCES:
...miss out on their chocolate beer pie!

IV: Agri-Adventures

Agritourism, markets, locavore must-dos, and farm-to-table experiences

Fort Collins' Farmers' Market Awesomeness

As you draw near, the distant sound of live music finds your ears, accented subtly by the melody of youthful laughter. As you start walking around, the positive energy is contagious, and the plethora of smiles and friendly faces seem to be putting off a near tangible electricity of happiness. Then comes the aromas wafting about, the smells of home-baked goodies flirting with your senses, while the scent of farm-fresh produce and eccentric food trucks carries your thoughts to a place you never want to leave.

Some sort of carnival? A happiness festival? A birthday party for earth? Nope... just a Colorado-style farmers' market!

The Markets

There are three primary markets—and one winter market—in town, all boasting a varied abundance of food/craft vendors, and each one being an indefectible (Sorry, running out of positive adjectives... did that seem forced? It means, "perfect or faultless") way to spend an afternoon...

- Fort Collins Farmers' Market
- Larimer County Farmers' Market (Old Town)
- Drake Road Farmers' Market
- Winter Farmers' Market
- (hosted by the Northern Colorado Food Cluster)

Looking for more local food? Check out the Fort Collins Food Co-op grocery store!

The Cooking Studio
Cooking Class

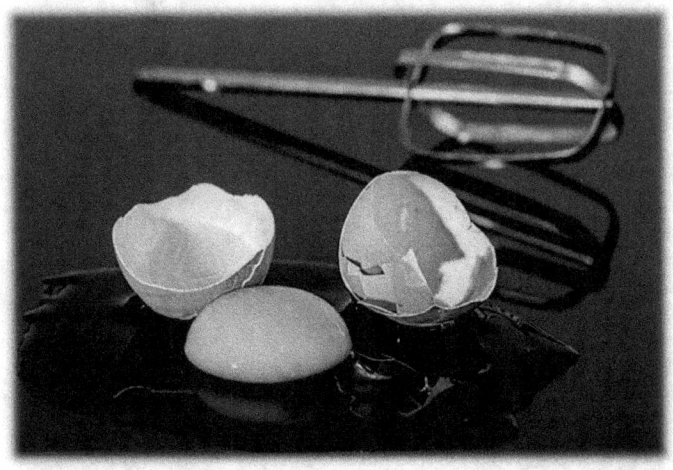

Eating out is awesome, but at the end of the day, food is like art... and while it's a beautiful thing to appreciate other people's creations, it will never replace getting hands on with your own food in your own kitchen. But YouTube has ads, cookbooks are boring, and nothing compares to the electricity of in-person learning... which is precisely why this "culinary playground" is so danged awesome! Whether you're a total newbie who can't boil water, or a seasoned veteran looking to hone a new skill, these guys offer classes to fit all skill levels, ages, and dietary preferences.

Food Tours!

TheMagicBusTours.com
"Farm-to-Table Tour"

FortCollinsTours.com
"Speakeasies & Spirits Tour"

Fort Collins Foodie Walk
*Self-guided exploration of
Fort Collin's finest culinary shops.*

LocalTableTours.com
*These guys offer all sorts of food tour optons in Fort Collins, Denver, and Boulder. I periodically work as one of their guides, so if you and a group ever want to go on an edible adventure with me, just shoot me an email!
Marjerison@Gmail.com*

Esh's
Crazy Food Bargins

Remember that one time when you were little and somehow you ended up at an arcade that had all-you-can-play games? For the first time in your life... your fun levels were uncapped, and for those glorious few hours the financial restrictions of a pocketful of quarters became a distant memory. That's sort of what this little grocery store is like! Isles full of past-date foods (still perfectly safe and delicious) of all kinds, from fresh produce and dairy to granola bars and drinks—with price tags a fraction of the norm.

I once got 10 avocados for 1$ ...see if you can beat that!

The Cupboard
Treats & (Kitchen) Toys

This place is a lot like Disney World... except that instead of roller coasters, there's every kitchen tool and accessory you could ever imagine; instead of Mickey Mouse and his friends to take pictures with, there's store clerks with an unparalleled knowledge of all things cooking; and instead of funnel cake and cotton candy, there's artisanal pantry-fillers and locally-made goodies.

Howling Cow Café
Farm Fresh Latte

A wise man once said: if you want the best glass of milk... go to the utter. No one knows for sure if this wise man was speaking literally or not, but if he was, I would have to disagree—milking a cow is both difficult and impractical to the point that it's irrelevant to the average milk drinker. So with that out, I found the next best thing for the ultimate latte... a coffee shop that sits a rock's throw from their own dairy farm!

> **Fun Fact:** *This same dairy farm is responsible for producing Noosa yogurt*

Ten Bears Winery
Local Wine Flight

"I can only describe an evening at Ten Bears Winery, as the most perfectly spectacular enjoyable beautifulness of all evenings in all eternity... times infinity."
—Almost Surely Someone

Not the kinda person who trusts spurious quotes? Fair enough... go see for yourself! As you sit outside, gazing over quaint rows of grape vines, slowly succumbing to the vineyard's meditative tranquility, delicately sipping through a variety of micro-batch wines, I'm sure you'll agree... there are few better ways to enjoy a Colorado summer evening.

The Growing Project
Pick-Your-Own Produce

Getting hands on is always better—it's that simple. Example, go YouTube a video of riding a bike. Now, go ride a bike. Which was more awesome? Exactly. Seriously though, getting hands on with your food is a beautiful thing. It builds community while encouraging food system sustainability, not to mention you get to experience the vibrant flavor-festival of freshly picked produce. Convinced? Check out this local non-profit's community gardens, where anyone is welcome to trade volunteer hours for PYO produce. Along with gardening, they offer classes, workshops, and various special events, with a plethora of more information (obviously) on their website: @ TheGrowingProject.org

 Jessup Farm Artisan Village
Everything Nice

From shopping to farm animals, this spot offers an overwhelming amount of options, so to help thwart the inevitable case of the "should-haves," I've conducted a rigorous study, narrowing down my personal must-tries:

1. *From the primary restaurant, The Farmhouse: try a homemade donut (flavors are ever changing—I got Piña Colada this time!).*
2. *From the direct-trade coffee roaster, Bindle: go for one of their single origin beans, prepared Aero Press style—a brew method both entertainingly unique, and capable of a mean cup of joe!*
3. *From the craft brewery, Barrel House: sip your way through their flavorful and novel <u>barrel-aged beers</u>… and here you thought barrel aging was just for wine and whiskey!*
4. *From the farm… a selfie with the chickens!*

Locally Loved
Farm Adventures

Garden Sweet
Pick-Your-Own Strawberries.

The Bartel's Farm
Participate in the annual pumpkin patch festivities.

Native Hill
*Have way too much fun at a canning party at **Native Hill**.*

Woolly Goat Farm
Educate yourself via a workshop, class, or "farm school."

Bonus

Spot:

Item:

What's it all about?
Take a photo and share with the rest of us! *#FoCoFoodist*

Bonus

Spot:

Item:

What's it all about?

Take a photo and share with the rest of us!
#FoCoFoodist

Names & Doodles

Names & Doodles

One Last Thing…

I worked hard to make this list entertaining and informative, but most importantly a tool to help awesome-ify your Fort Collins experience. If I was successful, I would truly appreciate it if you'd help spread the word via social media, body paint, word of mouth, carrier pigeon, etc.

I apologize in advance for any items that don't live up to your expectations. I'm always looking for feedback on your experiences with the list, as well as suggestions for items that you believe should be included in next year's edition—so don't hesitate to reach out!

If this book didn't live up to your expectations, e-mail me:

Marjerison@Gmail.com

So I can make things right.

Iver Marjerison

*After an exclusive diet of Qdoba and Ramwhiches during his first two years at CSU, Iver serendipitously stumbled into Old Town with an empty stomach... and has been mesmerized by the Fort Collins food scene ever since. Post graduation, he has gone on to get his MBA in Sustainable Food Systems, and works as a writer, educator, and marketing consultant through his company **Food Flow**. He also works as a wedding planner specializing in small weddings through his company **Colorado MicroWeddings**. While his passion is to help improve the sustainability of our global food system, he often— and gleefully—gets sidetracked hunting down and sharing edible adventures.*

IverMarjerison.com
Marjerison@gmail.com
@Iver.Marjerison

www.ingramcontent.com/pod-product-compliance
Lightning Source LLC
Chambersburg PA
CBHW051403290426
44108CB00015B/2133